My First Book of Poems
Coloring Book

EDITED BY
Victoria Fremont

ILLUSTRATED BY
Nina Barbaresi

DOVER PUBLICATIONS, INC.
New York

Bibliographical Note

My First Book of Poems Coloring Book is a new work, including previously published children's verse, first published by Dover Publications, Inc., in 1993.

International Standard Book Number: 0-486-27824-7

Manufactured in the United States of America
Dover Publications, Inc., 31 East 2nd Street, Mineola, N.Y. 11501

Note

This volume contains a sampling of the most familiar and acclaimed poems written for the very young. These verses are fun to read aloud and will provide young people with many hours of enjoyment. Specially selected to appeal to young people today, the dozens of poems in this book are accompanied by delightful illustrations designed to be colored in with pens, pencils or paints. After you read these poems and color in the pictures, you may use your imagination to create original works of your own!

Mr. Nobody

I know a funny little man,
   As quiet as a mouse,
Who does the mischief that is done
   In everybody's house!
There's no one ever sees his face,
   And yet we all agree
That every plate we break was cracked
   By Mr. Nobody.

'Tis he who always tears our books,
   Who leaves the door ajar,
He pulls the buttons from our shirts,
   And scatters pins afar;
That squeaking door will always squeak,
   For, prithee, don't you see,
We leave the oiling to be done
   By Mr. Nobody.

The finger marks upon the door
  By none of us are made;
We never leave the blinds unclosed,
  To let the curtains fade.
The ink we never spill; the boots
  That lying round you see
Are not our boots—they all belong
  To Mr. Nobody.

—ANONYMOUS

Mix a Pancake

Mix a pancake,
Stir a pancake,
　　Pop it in the pan;
Fry the pancake,
Toss the pancake—
　　Catch it if you can.

—Christina Rossetti

Antigonish

As I was going up the stair
I met a man who wasn't there;
He wasn't there again today—
I wish, I *wish*, he'd stay away.

—HUGHES MEARNS

I'm Nobody! Who Are You?

I'm nobody! Who are you?
Are you nobody, too?
Then there's a pair of us—don't tell!
They'd banish us, you know.

How dreary to be somebody!
How public, like a frog
To tell your name the livelong day
To an admiring bog!

—EMILY DICKINSON

The Grasshopper
and the Elephant

Way down South where bananas grow,
A grasshopper stepped on an elephant's
    toe.
The elephant said, with tears in his eyes,
"Pick on somebody your own size."

—Anonymous

9

Morning

Will there really be a morning?
  Is there such a thing as day?
Could I see it from the mountains
  If I were as tall as they?

Has it feet like water-lilies?
  Has it feathers like a bird?
Is it brought from famous countries
  Of which I have never heard?

Oh, some scholar! Oh, some sailor!
  Oh, some wise man from the skies!
Please to tell a little pilgrim
  Where the place called morning lies.

—EMILY DICKINSON

I Eat My Peas with Honey

I eat my peas with honey;
I've done it all my life.
It makes the peas taste funny,
But it keeps them on the knife.

—ANONYMOUS

Time to Rise

A birdie with a yellow bill
Hopped upon the window sill,
Cocked his shining eye and said:
"Ain't you 'shamed, you sleepy-head!"

—ROBERT LOUIS STEVENSON

Peter Piper

Peter Piper picked a peck of pickled
    peppers;
A peck of pickled peppers Peter Piper
    picked;
If Peter Piper picked a peck of pickled
    peppers,
Where's the peck of pickled peppers Peter
    Piper picked?

—ANONYMOUS

13

There Was a Crooked Man

There was a crooked man, and he walked a
crooked mile,
He found a crooked sixpence against a
crooked stile;
He bought a crooked cat, which caught a
crooked mouse,
And they all lived together in a little
crooked house.

—ANONYMOUS

The Purple Cow

I never saw a Purple Cow,
I never hope to see one;
But I can tell you, anyhow,
I'd rather see than be one.

—GELETT BURGESS

The Cow

The friendly cow all red and white,
  I love with all my heart:
She gives me cream with all her might,
  To eat with apple-tart.

She wanders lowing here and there,
  And yet she cannot stray,
All in the pleasant open air,
  The pleasant light of day;

And blown by all the winds that pass
  And wet with all the showers,
She walks among the meadow grass
  And eats the meadow flowers.

—ROBERT LOUIS STEVENSON

Animal Fair

I went to the animal fair,
The birds and beasts were there.
The big baboon by the light of the moon
Was combing his auburn hair.

The monkey he got drunk.
He stepped on the elephant's trunk.
The elephant sneezed
And fell on his knees,
And that was the end of the monk, the
    monk, the monk.
And that was the end of the monk.

—ANONYMOUS

The Squirrel

Whisky, frisky,
Hipperty hop,
Up he goes
To the tree top!

Whirly, twirly,
Round and round,
Down he scampers
To the ground.

—ANONYMOUS

A Bird

A bird came down the walk:
He did not know I saw;
He bit an angle-worm in halves
And ate the fellow, raw.

And then he drank a dew
From a convenient grass,
And then hopped sidewise to the wall
To let a beetle pass.

—EMILY DICKINSON

The Frog

What a wonderful bird the frog are—
When he stand, he sit almost;
When he hop, he fly almost
He ain't got no sense hardly;
He ain't got no tail hardly either.
When he sit, he sit on what he ain't got
    almost.

—ANONYMOUS

23

The Crocodile

How doth the little crocodile
  Improve his shining tail,
And pour the waters of the Nile
  On every golden scale!

How cheerfully he seems to grin,
  How neatly spreads his claws,
And welcomes little fishes in,
  With gently smiling jaws!

—LEWIS CARROLL

What Do They Do?

What does the bee do?
 Bring home honey.
And what does Father do?
 Bring home money.
And what does Mother do?
 Lay out the money.
And what does baby do?
 Eat up the honey.

—CHRISTINA ROSSETTI

Which Is the Way
to Somewhere Town?

Which is the way to Somewhere Town?
  Oh, up in the morning early;
Over the tiles and the chimney pots,
  That is the way, quite clearly.

And which is the door to Somewhere
    Town?
  Oh, up in the morning early;
The round red sun is the door to go
    through,
  That is the way, quite clearly.

—KATE GREENAWAY

There Was an Old Man
in a Tree

There was an Old Man in a tree,
Who was horribly bored by a bee;
   When they said, "Does it buzz?"
   He replied, "Yes, it does!
It's a regular brute of a bee!"

—EDWARD LEAR

Three Things to Remember

A Robin Redbreast in a cage
Puts all Heaven in a rage.

A skylark wounded on the wing
Doth make a cherub cease to sing.

He who shall hurt the little wren
Shall never be beloved by men.

—WILLIAM BLAKE

The Swing

How do you like to go up in a swing,
　Up in the air so blue?
Oh, I do think it the pleasantest thing
　Ever a child can do!

Up in the air and over the wall,
　Till I can see so wide,
Rivers and trees and cattle and all
　Over the countryside—

Till I look down on the garden green,
　Down on the roof so brown—
Up in the air I go flying again,
　Up in the air and down!

—ROBERT LOUIS STEVENSON

31

Autumn

The morns are meeker than they were,
  The nuts are getting brown;
The berry's cheek is plumper,
  The rose is out of town.

The maple wears a gayer scarf,
  The field a scarlet gown.
Lest I should be old-fashioned,
  I'll put a trinket on.

—EMILY DICKINSON

Who Has Seen the Wind?

Who has seen the wind?
  Neither I nor you:
But when the leaves hang trembling
  The wind is passing thro'.

Who has seen the wind?
  Neither you nor I:
But when the trees bow down their heads
  The wind is passing by.

—CHRISTINA ROSSETTI

My Shadow

I have a little shadow that goes in and out
    with me
And what can be the use of him is more
    than I can see.
He is very, very like me from the heels up
    to the head;
And I see him jump before me, when I
    jump into my bed.

The funniest thing about him is the way he
    likes to grow—
Not at all like proper children, which is
    always very slow;
For he sometimes shoots up taller like an
    india-rubber ball,
And he sometimes gets so little that there's
    none of him at all.

—ROBERT LOUIS STEVENSON

The Young Lady of Niger

There was a young lady of Niger
Who smiled as she rode on a Tiger;
  They came back from the ride
  With the lady inside,
And the smile on the face of the Tiger.

—Anonymous

On Digital Extremities

I'd Rather have Fingers than Toes;
I'd Rather have Eyes than a Nose;
  And As for my hair,
  I'm Glad it's all there;
I'll be Awfully Sad, when it Goes!

—GELETT BURGESS

Pippa's Song

The year's at the spring
And the day's at the morn;
Morning's at seven;
The hillside's dew-pearled;
The lark's on the wing;
The snail's on the thorn:
God's in his heaven—
All's right with the world!

—Robert Browning

There Was an Old Man with a Beard

There was an Old Man with a beard,
Who said, "It is just as I feared!
  Two Owls and a Hen,
  Four Larks and a Wren,
Have all built their nests in my beard!"

—EDWARD LEAR

There Was an Old Person Whose Habits

There was an Old Person whose habits
Induced him to feed upon rabbits;
   When he'd eaten eighteen,
   He turned perfectly green,
Upon which he relinquished those habits.

—EDWARD LEAR

A Young Lady of Norway

There was a Young Lady of Norway
Who casually sat in a doorway;
   When the door squeezed her flat,
   She exclaimed, "What of that?"
This courageous Young Lady of Norway.

—EDWARD LEAR

There Is a Young Lady, Whose Nose

There is a Young Lady, whose nose
Continually prospers and grows;
  When it grew out of sight,
  She exclaimed in a fright,
"Oh! Farewell to the end of my nose!"

—EDWARD LEAR

Hand-Clapping Rhyme

Did you eever iver ever
In your long-legged life,
See a long-legged sailor
Kiss his long-legged wife?

No, I neever niver never
In my long-legged life,
Saw a long-legged sailor
Kiss his long-legged wife!

—TRADITIONAL

There Was a Little Girl

There was a little girl,
And she had a little curl
  Right in the middle of her forehead.
When she was good
She was very, very good,
  And when she was bad she was horrid.

—ANONYMOUS

Fuzzy Wuzzy

Fuzzy Wuzzy was a bear;
Fuzzy Wuzzy had no hair.
So Fuzzy Wuzzy wasn't fuzzy. Was he?

—ANONYMOUS

The Moon

I see the moon,
And the moon sees me;
God bless the moon,
And God bless me.

—ANONYMOUS

I'm Glad

I'm glad the sky is painted blue,
    And the earth is painted green,
With such a lot of nice fresh air
    All sandwiched in between.

—ANONYMOUS

Jump-Rope Rhyme

"Hello, hello, hello, sir,
Meet me at the grocer."
"No sir."
"Why sir?"
"Because I have a cold, sir."
"Where did you get your cold, sir?"
"At the North Pole, sir."
"What were you doing there, sir?"
"Shooting polar bear, sir."
"Let me hear you sneeze, sir."
"Kachoo, kachoo, kachoo, sir."

—TRADITIONAL

At the Zoo

First I saw the white bear,
    Then I saw the black;
Then I saw the camel
    With a hump upon his back;
Then I saw the grey wolf,
    With mutton in his maw;
Then I saw a wombat
    Waddle in the straw;
Then I saw the elephant
    A-waving of his trunk;
Then I saw the monkeys—
    Mercy, how unpleasantly they—
Smelt!

—WILLIAM MAKEPEACE THACKERAY

The Little Elf

I met a little Elfman once,
  Down where the lilies blow.
I asked him why he was so small,
  And why he didn't grow.

He slightly frowned, and with his eye
  He looked me through and through—
"I'm quite as big for me," said he,
  "As you are big for you!"

—JOHN KENDRICK BANGS

Bed in Summer

In winter I get up at night
And dress by yellow candle-light.
In summer, quite the other way,
I have to go to bed by day.

I have to go to bed and see
The birds still hopping on the tree,
Or hear the grown-up people's feet
Still going past me in the street.

And does it not seem hard to you,
When all the sky is clear and blue,
And I should like so much to play,
To have to go to bed by day?

—Robert Louis Stevenson

Hopping Frog

Hopping frog, hop here and be seen,
  I'll not pelt you with stick or stone:
Your cap is laced and your coat is green;
  Goodbye, we'll let each other alone.

—Christina Rossetti

The Centipede

A centipede was happy quite,
   Until a frog in fun
Said, "Pray, which leg comes after which?"
This raised her mind to such a pitch,
She lay distracted in the ditch
   Considering how to run.

—ANONYMOUS

Midnight

Midnight's bell goes ting, ting, ting, ting,
ting,
Then dogs do howl, and not a bird does
sing
But the nightingale, and she cries twit,
twit, twit:
Owls then on every bough do sit;
Ravens croak on chimney's tops;
The cricket in the chamber hops,
    And the cats cry mew, mew, mew;
The nibbling mouse is not asleep,
But he goes peep, peep, peep, peep, peep,
    And the cats cry mew, mew, mew,
    And still the cats cry mew, mew, mew.

—THOMAS MIDDLETON

There Was an Old Lady of Chertsey

There was an Old Lady of Chertsey,
Who made a remarkable curtsey;
  She twirled round and round,
  Till she sank underground,
Which distressed all the people of Chertsey.

—EDWARD LEAR

The Crocodile

If you should meet a crocodile,
  Don't take a stick and poke him;
Ignore the welcome in his smile,
  Be careful not to stroke him.
For as he sleeps upon the Nile,
  He thinner gets and thinner;
And whene'er you meet a crocodile
  He's ready for his dinner.

—ANONYMOUS

I Asked My Mother

I asked my mother for fifty cents
To see the elephant jump the fence.
He jumped so high that he touched the sky
And never came back till the Fourth of July.

—ANONYMOUS

If a Woodchuck Would Chuck

How much wood would a woodchuck chuck
If a woodchuck could chuck wood?
He would chuck what wood a woodchuck
    would chuck,
If a woodchuck would chuck wood.

—ANONYMOUS